Bento Box

Bento Box

Poems by

Mackenzie Moore

Cover design by Shay Culligan
Cover art by Mackenzie Moore

ISBN: 978-1-952326-46-2

Kelsay Books
502 South 1040 East, A-119
American Fork, Utah, 84003

To Megan.

For always packing enough for the both of us

Acknowledgments

Bento Box is a container for pride, grief,
and the confusing shape of change.

Some of the poems in this collection appeared first in the following homes:

Variant Literature: "Drip"

The Northridge Review: "Thawing"

Mineral Lit: "Old Houses"

Lunch Ticket: "O'Hare"

TEJASCOVIDO: "Friday 13.3"

845 Press: "Maintenance"

To the many eyes for reading, and the many hands for nudging, the solidarity transcended zip codes. Thank you.

Contents

Drip   11
Primaries   13
Thawing   14
Half Price   17
Old Houses   19
Crumbs   21
O'Hare   24
Friday 13.3   26
Maintenance   28
Bag of Rice   29
Letter to My Young Bones   30
Chicago   31
Literacy   32

Drip

The rituals I keep
in quiet California
are small,
carry on packable:
grinding
measuring
boiling

When I don't
dictate the day
by virtue of grams
I wobble
into the morning
my continuity thrown off

I think of those
railroad kitchens
my same bare feet
married to cold tile
still grinding
measuring
boiling

I think of
Ira
of Mike
of Jia
building their word churches
back in New York

I was watered down
So I left
to spend long nights
roasting out the acrid bite
One day: silky stories
that go down smooth.

Primaries

RFK said
like it or not,
we live in interesting times

Pretty sure
that was in '66
Granted, he'd buried his brother
and stiffened his lip with Kefauver
Bobby himself had just
two more good years

Interesting,
but a sunny day
euphemism for terrifying

But what else
can you tell
a bunch of college kids
three years out
from little Teddy
leaving Chappaquiddick
and his conscience
at the bottom of a pond

Who is anyone
to say otherwise
when we believe
things will
All. Work. Out.

Hope,
rainy day real estate
as we sit on our
housing bubble.

Thawing

My friend told me
LA would thaw me
This is good
she said
tucking my scarf tighter
the brittleness of Chelsea
cutting through both our coats

Mhmm
I nodded
Suspicious.
But I wasn't one to talk
a glistening block of ice
sliding along
unable to be stopped
unable to sit still
unable to be touched

She wasn't wrong
I dripped for a solid year
leaving trails behind me
as I tried to acclimate
to the blinding light

This thawing though:
all the water has to go somewhere
That without the municipal pipes
dumping into the East River
you need to find
new storm drains

People in LA cry in their cars
there is no solidarity
like crying on the train
where someone will
shoot you *the glance*
that infinitesimal nod
We've been there,
you'll be okay

You cry in the sunshine
and it feels like a joke
Like the equipment van
parked on your street
will call wrap
so you can go back to
whatever it is you do

Your wish is granted
and so you stop thawing
before you even realize
You go out one morning
ready to wipe up
after your soggy footprints
but they're gone

Huh.
just like that
you nod,
Suspicious.
But you're preoccupied
picking at your skin
parched, papery

When did thawing
slip to drying
Could use some cold weather
But you can't go back to freezing—
surely, it would cause cracks.

Half Price

We're hitting pot holes
so I keep replacing
parts to make
the drive smoother

You hate my tiny car
and "maps"
keeps saying
there's an exit marked
"The going is still good"
But good God
we can't find it

You weren't on this
side of the country
when I was telling stories,
tales so convincing
I wasn't worthy of Love

Inches of life
sheared right off my laugh
leaving but scar tissue to
hint at the cracks of someone
just trying to Love

I'm not taking suggestions
but, I'm looking through
the windshield
at a sea of brake lights
remembering
how much it burns
when the air bag goes off

I'd like the ride to be
less of a haul
Because you found me
a little broken
but with good bones:

Half price.

Old Houses

I didn't really think about it
until it hit me
oh.
Oh.
There are a lot of women
with porcelain skin
and big, spacious laughs
between us

Distance is a little vacuum
you can't empty out
when you've had your fill
I want to say
it makes ya grow fonder
But:

You've told me things
in confidence
Sure, we all feel confident
with the lights on

This space though,
is letting the wind
whip through:
A big old house
settling into itself at night

You start hearing creaks
wondering what may be
poking around
Convinced you hear
some big, spacious laugh
coming for you
One foot
already on the stairs.

Crumbs

I:

The first year
the heaviness
disperses into little remnants,
emotional feta
crumbs left on every corner
south of 28th street

I am fragile with strangers
the Cooper Union post master
the children on the Q train
the Staten Island ferry tourists
we sit shoulder to shoulder
I hold their cameras,
I am too tired to pull away.

II:

The anger has taken root
I stack my obligations
in thick, protective layers
time is a commodity,
don't touch it

Come home,
flick off the light
hope nothing
shakes the detente
stuck in the cobwebs
for the next six hours
make my bed, all over, again.

III:

Uproot everything
to burn off the cobwebs
the phantom limb calls collect
from miles away
it warns: don't fail
your muscle memory now

At long last
found them: the arrows
back to the assembly line
of self-improvement
moving forward,
always forward
Forward Forward Forward.

IV:

I am tired again
the heaviness fortified,
like wool
I open my arms
to the pilling feeling
I expect will come

When it does,
I auction off the fragments
to the pockets of those I love
pull them in tight
kiss them goodbye
each time, one less piece
without a home.

V:

My voice, quieter
the frequency of yelling
as measured in years
like amber alerts
when they come out
the words alarm people

I get more tattoos
if only to prove
they won't ruin me
markers with which
to measure the tide
of years in past tense

I fall asleep
I wake up
a routine to bookend
flexing the scar tissue
dormant, rigid
but still, very much alive.

O'Hare

It's always the drive to the airport
when you look at me
merging concern from
the corner of your right eye
in my direction.
You're worried, you tell me
I look tired
I seem stressed
I didn't touch my wine.

It's always the drive to the airport
when you have me
buckled into a corner.
You're worried, you tell me
I'm working so much
I sound a little hollow
Honey.
It lingers
It's not sweet.

It's always the drive to the airport
when my reserves
to sit and listen patiently
have been run ragged
when the dull ache sets in
like bare feet
on concrete.

I sink into the seat
and don't point out
your habit
the one where you take everything
that keeps me up at night
emptying it out like a bag

picking up each grievance
to test the weight.
You set your findings back down
waving them off
like you went when it wasn't your turn.

It's always the drive to the airport
that I dampen the urge to tell you
your interrogations
drain the light out of me
like the kitchen tap
you still haven't fixed yet.

Friday 13.3

I crawled into bed
with a rice beer
the shop owner
claimed tasted
"Light"
"Clean."

I bought it before
we were told to go home
Stay Home.

It made me queasy,
so cloyed with sugar
that I put it down
rolled over
sobbed so hard
my chest buckled.

Concealer pooling down
into my contacts
I didn't wipe it
shouldn't wear it
because they said
Don't touch your face.

I wish I would've let
someone fix me
five years ago
when I started to rust.

The emptiness settled
across my chest
an X-ray blanket
with no results.

My boyfriend
may call it soon—
I don't know how we
can drag our leaking sandbag
into this future anymore.

Maintenance

Lying on the floor again
most nights
Most people
say "Okay"
Check the glossary,
could fall under
meaningless
exhaustion
Both. Yes, and:

Prostrate?
On laminate?
Sounds like that yellow light
fixed atop dash is on

Grinding?
Yes
Ticking?
Yes
Trouble starting?
Yes
Trouble stopping?
Yes

Hood tap, heavy sigh
I hear the jumper cables
before I see them
This '93 transmission
got problems

You park it
in the garage every night?
So what.
My friend, you need maintenance.

Bag of Rice

Left to my cocoon
more time to tend than
I've had in years

Yet: my green thumb is burned
& my plants are shriveled
like the dates I dragged out on
tip toe from the cupboard

I can't soak them in water
like I soak myself in Epsom salt,
hoping to expel
the briny sadness
that keeps the blood
flowing to my feet

Where is the Miracle Gro
for the holes I pock in my
apartment, pacing at midnight
who is coming to pull
me out of the tub
& pat coffee grounds
around my withering edges

Left to my own devices,
I'm pruny, so overwatered
it might be mistaken for
drowning

If you have a chance,
won't you dry me out—
shake off the excess and
sink me in rice.

Letter to My Young Bones

The discomfort,
each day as if you've
slept in jeans

Like sneaker tongues
sunken and lopsided
stiff tags to carve routes
down your torso
dried sleep pinning
shut the lids—
the evidence will stay

I know you had plans
not for nights out,
new things,
and relishing
no, quiet hours banked
to disappear
into the balm of minutiae

It will take years
of spin cycles to soften
Keep kicking out the creases.

Chicago

Assumption on Illinois Street
pawning off poinsettias till January
Give 'em a home
so you press the
toxic wilting plant
against your chest
keeping it alive
so it can see its shadow
on Groundhog Day

The thermostat:
passive chess for
one degree more—
let me win
I don't play anymore

Smoggy tailpipes protesting
the tax to the ferryman
the Hillside strangler
holds the keys to set you free

Just like:
Kennedy, Ike, and Dan Ryan
trying to teach you to slow down
forehead against cold glass
looking for the hideouts
you used to call home.

Literacy

Don't do [hard] drugs
stay away from sugar
dodge the powdered down grains
that rise back to life like Lazarus
into three stack, silver dollars
on Sunday mornings

Watch your liquor,
or, watch your mouth
with the liquor

No one said:
don't stop reading
watch yourself
before you lose

Yourself, now warm
to the numb disinterest—
the screens won't save you

My mom's mom
is rounding third base
on 90, risen to life
with the butter and smoke
of 1930 fused to her bones—
she keeps reading

It won't save you
but you might pocket
just enough to heal

Yourself, now immune
to the numb disinterest
as you rise back to life
on Sunday mornings,
like three stack, silver dollars.

About the Author

Mackenzie Moore is a writer and illustrator based in Los Angeles, by way of New York and the suburbs of Chicago.

She believes bagels heal most wounds.

www.ingramcontent.com/pod-product-compliance
Lightning Source LLC
Chambersburg PA
CBHW031155090426
42738CB00008B/1349